BOUGHT FOR MOM with
GIFT CERTIFICATE GIVEN TO
HER BY NICE RED HEAD
NURSE, ERIK, WHILE AT
CONDELL MEMORIAL HOSP.

WG

Grandmothers Are Forever

Grandmothers Are Forever

Compiled and Edited by Criswell Freeman

WALNUT GROVE PRESS
Nashville, TN 37205

ISBN 1-887655-88-3

The ideas expressed in this book are not, in all cases, exact quotations, as some have been edited for clarity and brevity. In all cases, the author has attempted to maintain the speaker's original intent. In some cases, material for this book was obtained from secondary sources, primarily print media. While every effort was made to ensure the accuracy of these sources, the accuracy cannot be guaranteed. For additions, deletions, corrections or clarifications in future editions of this text, please write WALNUT GROVE PRESS.

Printed in the United States of America
1 2 3 4 5 6 7 8 9 10 • 98 99 00 01 02

ACKNOWLEDGMENTS
The author gratefully acknowledges the helpful support of Angela Beasley, Dick and Mary Freeman, and Mary Susan Freeman.

For Virginia Criswell and Marie Freeman

& Angie Knight

MeMom, Mammy & Nanny

Forever

Table of Contents

Introduction

This book pays tribute to grandmothers everywhere. And with good cause. Grandmothers help reshape eternity through their influence on future generations. Come to think of it, without grandmothers, there would be no future generations to influence.

In my own case, I am continually blessed by the lives of two special women: Virginia Criswell (known to her worshipful grandkids as "MeMom") and Marie Freeman (a beloved and feisty centenarian known as "Mammy"). My grandmothers helped shape me in ways that I am only beginning to understand as I reach midlife. And the more I learn about myself, the more I understand the value of caring, loving, supportive grandparents.

So if you happen to be a grandmother, thank you for all you have done and continue to do. If you happen to be a grandchild sneaking a peak at Grandma's quotation book, remember that grandmothers are forever; and remember that all you are you owe to your grandmother ... in more ways than one.

1

Grandmothers Are...

The dictionary defines the word "grandmother" in simple, straightforward fashion: "the mother of one's father or mother." But thoughtful grandchildren know that the true meaning of the word "grandmother" can never be defined so easily.

A grandmother is usually asked to assume many roles: She is teacher, friend, confidante, baby-sitter, family historian, spiritual advisor, family counselor and short-order cook. A grandmother is the foundation of the family, often the glue that holds the clan together. She guides her children and grandchildren by serving as a role model and an advice-giver of last resort.

On the pages that follow, we pay tribute to those special women who keep grateful grandchildren thanking their lucky stars for their great grandmothers.

A grandparent is a
unique kind of emotionally
involved, part-time parent
without pressure.

Dr. Fitzhugh Dodson

Grandmother is just another name for love.

Old-Time Saying

Grandmothers are the bearers of tradition.
Judith Stevens-Long

A grandparent is like a wise elder,
more detached than a parent.
Richard Walker

If a family has no grandparent,
it has no jewel.
Chinese Proverb

Grandparents are the family watchdogs.
Lillian E. Troll

Grandparents are our living link to the past.

George Bush

We learn to be grandmothers, just as
we learn to be mothers.

Sheila Kitzinger

Grandparents are more patient,
more tolerant, more aware of little changes
in their grandchild.

Nancy Reagan

Grandma was a first-aid station who restored
us to health by her amazing faith.

Lillian Smith

I thank God for my grandmother who stood
on the word of God and lived with the spirit
of courage and grace.

Maya Angelou

Her children arise up, and call her blessed.

Proverbs 31: 28

If you would civilize
a man, begin with
his grandmother.

Victor Hugo

Almost all grandmothers agree that
grandparenting is easier than parenting.

Judith Stevens-Long

Becoming a grandmother brings
the satisfaction of giving and receiving love,
sometimes more freely and more generously
than ever before.

Shelia Kitzinger

The connection between grandparents and
grandchild is natural and second
in emotional power only to the bond
between parent and child.

Arthur Kornhaber

Being a grandmother is above all
a learning experience.

Sheila Kitzinger

Grandparents have a special kind of love.

Eda LeShan

A grandmother is a person who has time.

Anonymous child's definition

Happiness is being a grandmother.

Jan Stoop and Betty Southard

2

Grandchildren Are…

Grandchildren are a bountiful blessing to grandparents who, without direct parental control, can usually enjoy their offspring at a safe distance. Herein, we explore the joys of observing, teaching and loving the children's children. May they live happily ever after.

Posterity is the patriotic name for grandchildren.

Art Linkletter

Your children are
your investment.
Your grandchildren are
your dividends.

Anonymous

A child is the greatest poem ever known.
Christopher Morley

Children are our immortality — in them we see the story of our life written in a fairer hand.
Alfred North Whitehead

The birth of every new baby is God's vote of confidence in the future of man.
Imogene Fey

A baby is God's opinion that life should go on.
Carl Sandburg

Better many children than many riches.
Vietnamese Proverb

Perfect love does not sometimes come until the first grandchild.

Welsh Proverb

Love must be learned again and again; there is no end to it. Hate needs no instruction.

Katherine Anne Porter

Children must be valued
as our most priceless possession.

James Dobson

Give a little love to a child and you get
a great deal back.

John Ruskin

Every child's relationship with a close and
loving grandparent is unique.

Arthur Kornhaber

Here's my advice:
Make sure your children
and grandchildren know
you love them.

Barbara Bush

When a grandchild is born, all relationships
in the family shift and change.

Sheila Kitzinger

When you have a grandchild,
you have two children.

Yiddish Saying

Your sons weren't made to like you.
That's what grandchildren are for.

Jane Smiley

Little children, little troubles.
Big children, big troubles.

Yiddish Saying

One hour with a child is like a ten-mile run.

Joan Benoit Samuelson

There was never a child so lovely but
his mother was glad to get him asleep.

Ralph Waldo Emerson

Blessed be childhood, which brings down
something of heaven into the midst
of our rough earthliness.

Henri Frédéric Amiel

A sweet child is the sweetest thing in nature.

Charles Lamb

Wherever children are, there is the golden age.

Novalis

In the eyes of its grandmother, every beetle is a gazelle.

African Proverb

The secret of life is to skip having children and go directly to grandchildren.

Mell Lazarus

3

Love

A grandmother's love is a wonderful thing for grandmoms and grandkids alike. A grandchild who has been lucky enough to feel the secure love of a caring grandparent will never forget that experience. And a grandparent who feels the touch of an adoring grandchild is forever changed.

Love is the currency by which life is denominated, a currency that is multiplied as it is spent. And, as we all know, when it comes to this currency of love, grandmothers are among the biggest of the big-time spenders. Thank goodness!

The closest friends I have made all through life have been people who also grew up close to a loved and loving grandfather or grandmother.

Margaret Mead

A grandmother's love is like no other love in the world.

Old-Time Saying

Love doesn't make the world go round.
Love is what makes the ride worthwhile.

Franklin P. Jones

There is a net of love by which
you can catch souls.

Mother Teresa

Love is the river of life in the world.

Henry Ward Beecher

There is only one terminal dignity — love.

Helen Hayes

You haven't lived if you haven't loved.

Old-Time Saying

Love stretches your heart and makes you big inside.

Margaret Walker

Love is a multiplication.

Marjory Stoneman Douglas

Love doesn't just sit there like a stone; it has to be made, like bread; remade all the time, made anew.

Ursula K. Leguin

Perfect love means to love the one through whom one became unhappy.

Kierkegaard

Grumbling is the death of love.

Marlene Dietrich

Great loves too must be endured.

Coco Chanel

Confidence is the best proof of love.

Maria Edgeworth

There is nothing so loyal as love.

Alice Cary

Love can make any place agreeable.

Old-Time Saying

To love is to receive a glimpse of heaven.

Karen Sunde

You can give without loving,
   but you cannot love without giving.

Amy Charmichael

Love does not dominate; it cultivates.

Goethe

Love is shown by deeds, not words.

Philippine Proverb

To love abundantly is to live abundantly, and to love forever is to live forever.

Anonymous

He who finds not love finds nothing.

Spanish Proverb

Take away love and our earth is a tomb.

Robert Browning

Love is the only true freedom. It lets us cast off our false exteriors and be our real selves.

Susan Polis Schutz

Until I truly loved, I was alone.

Caroline Norton

Love is the master key which opens the gates of happiness.

Oliver Wendell Holmes, Sr.

Let your grandchildren
know, through words and
deeds, that the bond of
affection which attaches
the two of you to one
another can never
be broken.

Arthur Kornhaber

4

Home

It has been said that "home is where the heart is." But it must be added that a grandchild's *second* home is where grandmother is. Fortunate kids build lifelong memories around the fun and games at Grandmother's.

In this chapter, we examine some of the essential elements of a happy, functional home. And we learn what savvy grandmoms have known all the while: A real home is any building built upon a foundation of love.

A house is not a home.

Polly Adler

It takes a heap o' lovin'
in a house to make
it a home.

Edgar A. Guest

Home

Home, in one form or another,
is the great object of life.

Josiah Gilbert Holland

Everyone has, I think, in some quiet corner
of his mind, an ideal home waiting to become a
reality.

Paige Rense

I have been very happy with my homes,
but homes really are no more than the people
who live in them.

Nancy Reagan

Home is not a way station:
It is the profession of faith in life.

Sol Chaneles

It takes a hundred men to make an
encampment, but one woman to make a home.

Robert Ingersoll

The woman who creates
and sustains a home
is a creator second
only to God.

Helen Hunt Jackson

Home — that blessed word which opens
to the human heart the most perfect glimpse
of Heaven.

Lydia M. Child

A house is no home unless it contains food
and fire for the mind as well as for the body.

Margaret Fuller

Make two homes for thyself: one actual
home and another spiritual home which thou
art to carry with thee always.

St. Catherine of Siena

Home ought to be our clearinghouse,
the place from which we go forth lessoned
and disciplined, and ready for life.

Kathleen Norris

Home is any four walls that enclose
the right person.

Helen Rowland

Home is where
thy heart is.

Pliny the Elder

Home wasn't built in a day.

Jane Ace

5

Family

Grandmothers, having raised the children who raise the children, possess special insights into family life. So when it comes to matters of house and home, wise kids and grandkids seek the advice of their clan's most experienced mother.

The observations, tips and common-sense advice in this chapter are intended for families everywhere. And if these words sound suspiciously like those uttered by grandmother, so be it. After all, grandmother knows best.

The family — that dear octopus from whose tentacles we never quite escape, nor, in our inmost hearts, ever quite wish to.

Dodie Smith

Family life is the source of the greatest human happiness.

Robert J. Gavinghurst

Healthy families are our greatest national resource.

Dolores Curran

The strength of a nation derives from the integrity of the home.

Confucius

A family is a place where
principles are hammered
and honed on the anvil
of everyday living.

Charles Swindoll

Family is the we of me.

Carson McCullers

A family is a school of duties...founded on love.

Felix Adler

Call it a clan, call it a network, call it a tribe,
call it a family. Whatever you call it,
whoever you are, you need one.

Jane Howard

The happiest moments of my life have been
spent in the bosom of my family.

Thomas Jefferson

A happy family is but an earlier heaven.

Sir John Bowring

Whoever is ashamed of his family
will have no luck.

Yiddish Proverb

No kingdom divided can stand —
neither can a household.

Christine de Pisan

Better a hundred enemies outside the house
than one inside.

Arabian Proverb

When the whole family is together,
the soul is in place.

Russian Proverb

Keep your family from the abominable practice of backbiting.

The Old Farmer's Almanac, 1811

A successful marriage requires falling in love
many times, always with the same person.

Mignon McLaughlin

All men are different. All husbands
are the same.

Old-Time Saying

A successful marriage is not a gift;
it is an achievement.

Ann Landers

$\mathbf{M}$arriage is a covered dish.

Swiss Proverb

$\mathbf{M}$ost men need more love than they deserve.

Marie von Ebner-Eschenbach

$\mathbf{W}$hen a marriage works, nothing on earth
can take its place.

Helen Gahagan Douglas

A bonus of being a grandmother is being
with babies and toddlers — and rediscovering
the delights of play.

Shelia Kitzinger

Grandparents are the living link
to the family's past.

Arthur Kornhaber

Govern a family as you would cook
a small fish — very gently.

Chinese Proverb

6

The Younger Generation

Every generation is the same, only different. But sometimes, parents are simply too close to the firing line to realize that their kids are not so unlike themselves. Mom and dad may panic, fearing that their children are irresponsible, strange or worse. What's needed is perspective. And who better to provide this perspective than grandmother? After all, she's a card-carrying member of the generation that has "seen it all" and lived to tell about it.

Grandparents understand that the more kids change, the more they remain the same. So parents take notice: Your children have the same hopes and dreams that you had at their age. But as for the hairstyles and clothing, well that's an entirely different matter.

Youth is the time of life when one believes
he is immortal.

William Hazlitt

Youth is wholly experimental.

Robert Louis Stevenson

Youth, even in its sorrows, always has
a brillancy of its own.

Victor Hugo

Beautiful is youth because
it never comes again.

George Jean Nathan

When you're young, the silliest notions seem
the greatest achievements.

Pearl Bailey

Children are all foreigners.

Ralph Waldo Emerson

Every age has its own follies.

American Saying

The life of children, as much as that
of intemperate men, is wholly governed
by their desires.

Aristotle

Adolescence can be a time of turmoil and
turbulence. Rebellion against authority and
convention is to be expected.

Haim Ginott

There is no sinner like a young saint.

Aphra Behn

We are none of us
infallible — not even
the youngest of us.

W. H. Thompson

No man knows he is young while he is young.

Lord Chesterfield

The excesses of our youths are drafts upon
our old age, payable with interest
about thirty years after date.

Charles Caleb Colton

It's a shame that we cannot have all the wisdom
one is ever to possess in the beginning.

Zora Neale Hurston

Childhood is never troubled with foresight.

Fanny Burney

Youth is the time to go flashing from one end
of the world to the other, both in mind
and body.

Robert Louis Stevenson

The modern child will answer you back
before you've said anything.

Laurence J. Peter

Like its politicians and its wars, society has
the teenagers it deserves.

J. B. Priestley

A child becomes an adult when he realizes
that he has a right not only to be right
but to be wrong.

Thomas Szasz

A boy becomes an adult about three years before you think he does and about two years after he thinks he does.

Lewis B. Hershey

With teen-agers and
their music in the house,
I can only say one thing:
"Thank God for a
hearing impediment."

Liz Carpenter

Youth is a fever of the mind.

La Rochefoucauld

A cynical young person is almost the saddest
sight to see because it means that he or she
has gone from knowing nothing
to believing in nothing.

Maya Angelou

You know children are growing up when
they start asking questions that have answers.

John J. Plomp

Nature makes boys and girls lovely to look
upon so they can be tolerated until they
acquire some sense.

William Lyon Phelps

It is amazing how quickly the kids learn to
drive a car, yet are unable to understand the
lawn mower, snow blower or vacuum cleaner.

Ben Bergor

There are three ways to get something:
do it yourself, employ someone, or forbid
your children to do it.

Monta Crane

Young folks will have their own way.

Martha Washington

Teen is a four letter word.

Popular Saying

Every generation revolts
against its parents and
makes friends with
its grandparents.

Lewis Mumford

In general, my children refuse to eat anything that hasn't danced on TV.

Erma Bombeck

Don't panic even during the storms
of adolescence. Better times are ahead.

James Dobson

Don't limit a child to your own learning
for he was born in another time.

Rabbinic Saying

You can learn many things from children.
How much patience you have, for instance.

Franklin P. Jones

My interest in young people is in rumpling
their brains as you might rumple
a good head of hair.

Robert Frost

We cannot always build the future for our
youth, but we can build our youth
for the future.

Franklin D. Roosevelt

If you can give your offspring only one gift, let it be Enthusiasm.

Bruce Barton

Parents, grandparents
and children each have
something to give
each other.

Fitzhugh Dodson

We've had bad luck with our kids — they've all grown up.

Christopher Morley

It's hard to know where
one generation ends and
the other begins. But it's
somewhere around
nine o'clock at night.

Charles Ruffing

7

Life

Life is a great mystery, except of course, to grandmothers. Somehow, somewhere, grandmothers figured things out. Thankfully, grandmoms are always willing to share their hard-earned knowledge — if the younger generation is willing to slow down long enough to listen.

This chapter contains grandmotherly advice about life. Kids, grandkids, great-grandkids, even casual bystanders, please take notice!

Life is a succession of moments,
to live each one is to succeed.

Corita Kent

It is more important to live the life one wishes
to live, and to go down with it if necessary, quite
contentedly, than live more profitable
but less happily.

Marjorie Kinnan Rawlings

Two things everybody's got to do for themselves:
They've got to trust God and they've got to find
out about living for themselves.

Zora Neale Hurston

"Now" is the watchword of the wise.

Charles Haddon Spurgeon

Yesterday is a canceled check, and tomorrow
is a promissory note. But today is cash,
ready for us to spend in living.

Barbara Johnson

Each day comes
bearing its own gifts.
Untie the ribbons.

Ruth Ann Schabacker

It is not how many years
we live, but what we
do with them.

Evangeline Cory Booth

Every day is a messenger of God.

Russian Proverb

We are tomorrow's past.

Mary Webb

Don't anticipate the happiness of tomorrow.
Discover it today.

Ella Wheeler Wilcox

I could never be content to simply look on.
Life was meant to be lived. We must never,
for any reason, turn our backs on life.

Eleanor Roosevelt

Life is a party; you join after its started and
you leave before its finished.

Elsa Maxwell

If you wish to live, you must first attend
your own funeral.

Katherine Mansfield

It's never to late — in fiction or in life —
to revise.

Nancy Thayer

Life is right now.

Barbara Bush

Every hour is a stranger to you —
until you live it.

Zora Neale Hurston

To live is to fight, to suffer and to love.

Elizabeth Leseur

God has a plan for all of us, but He expects us to do our share of the work.

Minnie Pearl

Life

It is important to stay close enough to the
pulse of life to feel its rhythm, to be comforted
by its steadiness, to know that life is vital,
and one's own living a torn fragment
of the larger cloth.

Marjorie Kinnan Rawlings

The greater part of our happiness depends
on our disposition and not our circumstances.

Martha Washington

It's not the load that breaks you down;
it's the way you carry it.

Lena Horne

Life is a stage I am going through.

Ellen Goodman

Surely the consolation prize of old age
is finding out how few things are worth
worrying over.

Dorothy Dix

Life is what we make it.
Always has been;
always will be.

Grandma Moses

Life is partly what me make it and partly
what is made by the friends we choose.

Chinese Proverb

The fingers of God touch your life
when you touch a friend.

Mary Dawn Hughes

The best mirror is a trusted, old friend.

Old-Time Saying

Real friendship is a slow grower.

Lord Chesterfield

It is great to have friends when one is young,
but indeed it is still more so when you are
getting old. When we are young, friends are,
like everything else, a matter of course. In the
old days we know what it means to have them.

Edvard Grieg

Happy is he to whom, in the maturer season
of life, there remains one tried and
constant friend.

Anna Letitia Barbauld

Old friends are best unless you catch
a new one fit to make an old one out of.

Sarah Orne Jewett

Remorse is the poison of life.

Charlotte Brontë

Wisdom means not making the same mistakes over and over again.

Jessica Tandy

Never fear shadows. They simply mean there's a light shining somewhere.

Ruth E. Renkel

The life that doesn't have a sense
of responsibility to something broader
than oneself is not much of a life.

Gail Sheehy

Life begets life. Energy creates energy.
It is by spending oneself that one becomes rich.

Sarah Bernhardt

We can learn so much from vital older
women who live their passions
with purpose and direction.

Gail Sheehy

Love the moment and the energy of the moment will be spread beyond all boundaries.

Corita Kent

The spiritual eyesight improves
as the physical eyesight declines.

Plato

On the human chessboard, all moves
are possible.

Miriam Schiff

What we are is God's gift to us.
What we become is our gift to God.

Eleanor Powell

8

Memories

It has been said that memory is the thing we forget with. But some memories are simply too priceless to lose. Happy remembrances of days gone by compose the fabric of life; they make us who we are. Other memories, those that breed bitterness or regret, are best discarded with vigor and haste.

The lessons in this chapter teach us that a retentive memory can be a blessing or a curse, depending upon how it is used. So all of us are advised to do what savvy grandmothers do: We should practice the art of memory management. Because we can never be fully contented until we remember to forget the things that don't need remembering. And vice versa.

To be able to enjoy one's past is to live twice.

Martial

Memory moderates prosperity, decreases adversity, controls youth and delights old age.

Lactantius Firmianus

No man can know where he is going unless he knows exactly where he's been.

Maya Angelou

Look at the past. Don't hide from it. It will not catch you if you don't repeat it.

Pearl Bailey

Lord, keep my memory green.

Charles Dickens

Remember childhood visions.

Mary McLeod Bethune

Praising what is lost
      makes the remembrance dear.
           William Shakespeare

Time...our youth...it never really goes,
      does it? It is all held in our minds.
           Helen Hoover Santmyer

Memory is a painter; it paints pictures
           of the past.
           Grandma Moses

Memory is the diary we all carry within us.
           Mary H. Waldrip

The little present must not be allowed wholly
      to elbow the great past out of our view.
           Andrew Lang

God gave us memories that we might have roses in December.

James M. Barrie

Old friends are the great blessing of one's
later years. They have a memory of the same
events and have the same mode of thinking.

Horace Walpole

Friends fill the memory with sweet things.

Martha Washington

There's no friend like someone who has
known you since you were five.

Anne Stevenson

May I forget what ought to be forgotten;
and recall unfailingly all that ought
to be recalled.

Laura Palmer

The companions of our childhood always
possess a certain power over our minds.

Mary Shelley

Middle age is when you've met so many people that every new person you meet reminds you of someone else.

Ogden Nash

Women and elephants never forget.

Dorothy Parker

A retentive memory may be a good thing,
but the ability to forget is the true token
of greatness.

Elbert Hubbard

Make it a rule of life never to regret and
never look back. Regret is an appalling waste
of energy; you can't build on it; it is only good
for wallowing in.

Katherine Mansfield

The things we remember best are those
better forgotten.

Baltasar Gracián

How we remember, what we remember,
and why we remember form the most personal
map of our individuality.

Christina Baldwin

In memory each of us is an artist;
each of us creates.

Patricia Hampt

Some folks never exaggerate — they just
remember big.

Audrey Snead

My grandmothers are full of memories.

Margaret Walker

A grandparent's memories,
those tales of times past,
. that seasoned view
of the world — these are
priceless gifts which the
grandparent alone can
offer their grandchildren.

Arthur Kornhaber

If I could remember your name, I'd ask you where I left my keys.

Bumper Sticker

2

Raising Grandkids

Most grandparents help raise their grandchildren at arm's length. In such cases, a little distance can be a very healthy thing. Because parents' parents are usually somewhat removed from the daily grind of child-rearing, they can offer counsel with a certain degree of objectivity. Such levelheaded advice is badly needed since parental objectivity, as we all know, is a commodity much rarer than gold.

In this chapter, we examine the ways that grandparents make a difference in the lives of their grandkids — a big difference.

Can grandmas make a difference in the lives of their grandchildren? Absolutely, but it takes energy and love.

Jan Stoop and Betty Southard

The role of teacher is one
of the most important
for any grandparent.

Arthur Kornhaber

Helping our children is often the best way
to help our grandchildren.

Eda LeShan

Grandmothers especially are frequently
called on to be a mother's personal
support system.

Arthur Kornhaber

Grandmothers can model love
in a very special way.

Jan Stoop and Betty Southard

A good-listener grandma tries to hear
the feeling behind the words that are spoken.

Jan Stoop and Betty Southard

For baby-sitting grandparents, love and exhaustion go hand in hand.

Eda LeShan

If grandparents want to have a meaningful
and constructive role, they must learn that
becoming a grandparent is *not* having a second
chance at parenthood!

Eda LeShan

Never tell your children how to raise
their children.

Fitzhugh Dodson

An important goal for grandparents
is not to compete with parents.

Eda LeShan

Very rarely will you make a mistake
by keeping quiet about something concerning
your grandchildren.

Fitzhugh Dodson

The secret of dealing successfully with a child is not to be its parent.

Mell Lazarus

A child's education should begin at least
a hundred years before he is born.
Oliver Wendell Holmes, Sr.

A great gift to one's child is knowledge.
Christine de Pisan

Better to have education than wealth.
Welsh Proverb

Let us continue toward educating character.
Ida B. Wells

Inspire youngsters to develop the talent
they possess.
Augusta Savage

Learning in childhood is like engraving
on a rock.

Arabian Proverb

As the twig is bent, so the tree grows.

Virgil

Trees bend only when young.

Jewish Saying

Wherever children are learning,
there dwells the Divine Presence.

Old Saying

When the pupil is ready, the teacher will come.

Chinese Saying

Those who are lifting the world upward
and onward are those who encourage
more than criticize.

Elisabeth Harrison

Reprove privately. Commend publicly.

Solan

The hearts of small children are delicate organs.

Carson McCullers

Children need love, especially when they
do not deserve it.

Harold S. Hulbert

Kind words can be short and easy to speak,
but their echoes are truly endless.

Mother Teresa

Listen! Encourage. Say something.
Do something. Be yourself. Love.

Dale Turner

The whole art of teaching is only the art of
awakening the natural curiosity of young minds
for the purpose of satisfying it afterwards.

Anatole France

Teaching is the art of assisting discovery.

Mark Van Doren

Children have to be educated, but they also
have to be left to educate themselves.

Abbé Dimnet

Education is not filling a pail,
but lighting a fire.

William Butler Yeats

Children have more need of models
than critics.

Joseph Joubert

Example is the school of mankind and
they will learn at no other.

Burke

Children have never been very good at
listening to their elders, but they have
never failed to imitate them.

James Baldwin

Children are very much aware of integrity;
when they see it they know it, though they
wouldn't know the word.

Eudora Weltry

We teach who we are.

John Gardner

Little children have big ears.

American Saying

He who lives well is the best teacher.

Cervantes

Education is life, not books.

African Proverb

Children are like clocks; they must be allowed to run.

James Dobson

To teach good behavior one wisely understands that young people must play and laugh.

Christine de Pisan

Take responsibility for the future of society
by raising responsible children.

Kaye Gibson

The most deprived children are those
who have to do nothing in order to get what
they want.

Sydney J. Harris

Do not handicap your children
by making their lives easy.

Lazarus Long

At every step the child should be allowed
to meet the real experiences of life; the thorns
should never be plucked from his roses.

Ellen Key

Never help a child with a task at which
he feels he can succeed.

Maria Montessori

You must teach your children to dream
with their eyes open.

Harry Edwards

Teach a child good manners during babyhood.

Nachman of Bratslav

Loving a child doesn't mean giving in to all
his whims; to love him is to bring out the best
in him, to teach him to love what is difficult.

Nadia Boulanger

Never argue with a child or a fool.

American Saying

Remember, when they have a tantrum,
don't have one of your own.

Judith Kurisansky

Good grandparenting begins early,
long before the birth of the first grandchild.

Arthur Kornhaber

When women talk about their own
grandmothers, the thing they value most was
the grandmother's willingness to listen.

Sheila Kitzinger

When you are dealing with a child,
keep your wits about you and sit on the floor.

Austin O'Malley

Was there ever a grandparent tired after
a day of minding noisy youngsters, who hasn't
felt the Lord knew what he was doing when
he gave little children to young people?

Joe E. Wells

Don't take up someone's time talking about
the smartness of your grandchildren. He wants
to talk about the smartness of his.

E. W. Howe

10

Forever Young

Youth is transitory, but a youthful spirit need never grow old. On the pages that follow, we consider a checklist of proven ways to retain or to regain that youthful spirit.

The ideas in this chapter compose the road map to a bubbling fountain of youth that exists within all of us. It is a fountain of our own construction; how we drink depends upon how we think.

Grandparenting is a marvelous opportunity to keep alive, alert, growing and giving.

Fitzhugh Dodson

Youth has no age.

Pablo Picasso

Life before 50 is nothing but a warm-up.

Advertisement for AARP

We turn not older with years, but newer
every day.

Emily Dickinson

Though it sounds absurd, it is true to say
I felt younger at sixty than I felt at twenty.

Ellen Glasgow

My interest is in the future because
I'm going to spend the rest of my life there.

Charles F. Kettering

To me, old age is always fifteen years older
than I am.

Bernard Baruch

Live your life and forget your age.

Frank Bering

If wrinkles must be written upon our brows,
let them not be written upon the heart.
The spirit should never grow old.

James A. Garfield

A man is not old until regrets take the place
of his dreams.

John Barrymore

Whatever wrinkles I got, I enjoyed
getting them.

Ava Gardner

I feel more at peace with myself than
when I was an ambitious young woman.

Jessica Tandy

You can't help getting older,
but you don't have to get old.

George Burns

Age is a case of mind over matter.
If you don't mind, it doesn't matter.

Jack Benny

It's not how old you are, but how you are old.

Marie Dressler

Age is all imagination. Ignore years and
they will ignore you.

Ella Wheeler Wilcox

Aging is a timeless ascent. As power diminishes,
we grow toward the light.

May Sarton

Nobody ought to be too old to improve.

Anna Letitia Barbauld

You don't grow old; when you cease to grow,
you are old.

Charles Judson Herrick

If we don't change, we don't grow.
If we don't grow, we are not really living.

Gail Sheehy

Only in growth, reform and change,
paradoxically enough, is true security found.

Anne Morrow Lindbergh

You can't turn back the clock.
But you can wind it up again.

Bonnie Prudden

The secret to longevity is keeping active
all the time.

Milton Berle

Keeping busy is the answer.

Marjory Stoneman Douglas
On her 100th birthday

Painting is not important. The important thing
is keeping busy.

Grandma Moses

Youth is a gift of nature; age is a work of art.

Anonymous

Aging slowly does not mean doing battle
with the passing years. It means enjoying them to
the hilt.

Myron Brenton

The most fulfilled older people maintain
a state of mind that, rather than clinging
fearfully to the past, accepts change
and encourages growth.

Connie Goldman and Richard Mahler

Activity does not wear out the human machine
and spirit...inactivity does.

Garson Kanin

The excitement of learning separates you
from old age. As long as you're learning,
you're not old.

Rosalyn S. Yalow

Age is bothersome only when you stop
to coddle it.

Maurice Chevalier

As soon as you feel too old to do a thing, do it.

Margaret Deland

Change is the constant, the signal for rebirth,
the egg of the phoenix.

Christina Baldwin

There are very few things you can do to defy
the aging process. Keeping your hopes alive
is definitely one of them.

Stanley H. Cath

Of all the things you wear, your expression
is the most important.

Janet Lane

Wrinkles should merely indicate
where smiles have been.

Mark Twain

There's the beauty of age, more profound, more complete. It forms a fine patina that only life and living can impart.

Karen Westerberg Reyes

The first forty years of life give us the text:
the next thirty supply the commentary.

Schopenhauer

In youth we learn. In age we understand.

Marie Ebner-Eschenbach

The evening of life brings with it its lamp.

Joseph Joubert

All that I know I learned after I was thirty.

Georges Clemenceau

Middle age is when you don't have
to have fun to enjoy yourself.

Franklin P. Jones

Anyone who keeps the ability to see beauty
never grows old.

Franz Kafka

All that is good in man lies in youthful
feeling and mature thought.

Joseph Joubert

I never feel age. If you have creative work,
you don't have age or time.

Louise Nevelson

Do not deprive me of my age.
I have earned it.

May Sarton

You are only young once, and if you work
it right, once is enough.

Joe E. Lewis

You stay young as long as you can learn,
acquire new habits and suffer contradictions.

Marie von Ebner-Eschenbach

It's the most unhappy people
who most fear change.

Mignon McLaughlin

The person who has lived the most is not
the one with the most years but the one
with the richest experiences.

Jean Jacques Rousseau

Look up and not down; look forward and
not back; look out and not in; and lend a hand.

Edward Everett Hale

Her grandmother, as she gets older,
is not fading but rather becoming
more concentrated.

Paulette Bates Alden

11

Grandmother's Advice

Who knows more than Grandmother? Nobody! And if you don't believe it, just ask her. So we conclude with a potpourri of wisdom that would make any grandmother proud. Enjoy!

We carry the seeds of happiness with us
wherever we go.

Martha Washington

Always keep that happy attitude.
Pretend that you are holding
a beautiful fragrant bouquet.

Candice M. Pope

Live each day as it comes, and don't borrow
trouble by worrying about tomorrow.

Dorothy Dix

Each day, look for a kernel of excitement.

Barbara Johnson

Talk happiness. The world is sad enough
without your woe.

Ella Wheeler Wilcox

I never really look for things. I accept whatever
God throws my way. Whichever way God
turns my feet, I go.

Pearl Bailey

Faith can put a candle in the darkest night.

Margaret Sangster

Without faith nothing is possible. With it,
nothing is impossible.

Mary McLeod Bethune

To eat bread without hope is still slowly
to starve to death.

Pearl Buck

Sad soul, take comfort nor forget,
The sunrise never failed us yet.

Celia Thaxter

One thing that doesn't abide by majority rule
is a person's conscience.

Harper Lee

If you listen to your conscience, it will serve
you as no other friend you'll ever know.

Loretta Young

Dignity is like a perfume; those who use it
are scarcely conscious of it.

Queen Christina of Sweden

When young people ask me how I made it,
I say, "It's absolutely hard work.
Nobody's gonna wave a magic wand."

Loretta Lynn

All our lives we are preparing to be something
or somebody, even if we don't know it.

Katherine Anne Porter

Everybody must learn
this lesson somewhere —
that it costs something
to be what you are.

Shirley Abbott

It's up to each of us to contribute something
to this sad and wonderful world.

Eve Arden

When you cease to contribute,
you begin to die.

Eleanor Roosevelt

Service is the rent you pay for room
on this earth.

Shirley Chisholm

Believe that your tender, loving thoughts
and wishes for good have the power to help the
struggling souls of earth rise higher.

Ella Wheeler Wilcox

This is happiness; to be dissolved
into something complete and great.

Willa Cather

Happiness is nothing but everyday living
seen through a veil.

Zora Neale Hurston

Jealousy is the most dreadfully involuntary
of all sins.

Iris Murdoch

Anger makes us all stupid.

Johanna Spyri

Envy is like a disease — it consumes the soul.

Jewish Proverb

Keep what is worth keeping and, with the
breath of kindness, blow the rest away.

Dinah Maria Murlock Craik

You've got to continue to grow, or you're just like last night's cornbread — stale and dry.

Loretta Lynn

I tell everybody to travel and not get married too soon.

Moms Mabley

The search for instant gratification is harmful.

Shirley Ann Grau

The best time to make friends is before you need them.

Ethel Barrymore

Take the back roads instead of the highways.

Minnie Pearl

The end is nothing.
The road is all.

Willa Cather

Charm is simply this: the golden rule,
  good manners, good grooming, good humor,
  good sense, good habits, and a good outlook.

Loretta Young

The best things you can give your children,
  next to good habits, are good memories.

Sydney J. Harris

Good manners will often take people where
neither money nor education will take them.

Fanny Jackson Coppin

Make beauty a familiar guest.

Mary Howitt

Revel in the exquisite beauty of the scenery
in springtime.

Pauline DeCara deuc Heyward

A woman is like a tea bag. You never know
how strong she is until she gets into hot water.

Eleanor Roosevelt

If you think you can, you can.
If you think you can't, you're right.

Mary Kay Ash

My grandmother used to say a day is wasted
if you don't fall over at least once with laughter.

Luci Swindoll

Treat the world well. It was not given to you
by your parents but lent to you
by your children.

Ida B. Wells

Grandmothers always come up with advice,
which is given whether you need it or not.

Rita Bourke

If you don't want your children to hear what
you're saying, pretend you're talking to them.

E. C. McKenzie

I have found the best way to give advice
to your children is to find out what they want
and then advise them to do it.

Harry S. Truman

Sources

Sources

About the Author

Criswell Freeman is a Doctor of Clinical Psychology living in Nashville, Tennessee. He is the author of *When Life Throws You a Curveball, Hit It* and *The Wisdom Series* from WALNUT GROVE PRESS. Dr. Freeman is also the host of *Wisdom Made in America*, a nationally syndicated daily radio program.

About Wisdom Books

Wisdom Books chronicle memorable quotations in an easy-to-read style. Written by Criswell Freeman, this series provides inspiring, thoughtful and humorous messages from entertainers, athletes, scientists, politicians, clerics, writers and renegades. Each title focuses on a particular region or area of special interest.

Combining his passion for quotations with extensive training in psychology, Dr. Freeman revisits timeless themes such as perseverance, courage, love, forgiveness and faith.

"Quotations help us remember the simple yet profound truths that give life perspective and meaning," notes Freeman. "When it comes to life's most important lessons, we can all use gentle reminders."